58 Collected Poems of Richard W. Moyer

All rights reserved. No part of this book shall be reproduced or transmitted in any form or by any means, electronic, mechanical, magnetic, photographic including photocopying, recording or by any information storage and retrieval system, without prior written permission of the publisher. No patent liability is assumed with respect to the use of the information contained herein. Although every precaution has been taken in the preparation of this book, the publisher and author assume no responsibility for errors or omissions. Neither is any liability assumed for damages resulting from the use of the information contained herein.

Copyright © 2010 by Richard W. Moyer

A Cat at the Battle of Waterloo reprinted courtesy of Free Verse magazine.
Straight Up reprinted courtesy of Ibbetson Street.
An Advertising Executive Runs the Cross Country reprinted courtesy of the Endicott Review.
Artillery Practice reprinted courtesy of the Endicott Review.
Feline Portrait reprinted courtesy of Free Verse.
Grim Ending reprinted courtesy of Nerve Cowboy.
Movies Youngstown Ohio 1940 reprinted courtesy of the Endicott Review.
A Murad Cigarette reprinted courtesy of the Endicott Review.
My Psychiatrist reprinted courtesy of the Mad Poets Review.
No Entrance reprinted courtesy of Nerve Cowboy.
What Was I Thinking About reprinted courtesy of Free Verse.

ISBN 0-7414-5917-5

Printed in the United States of America

Published May 2010

INFINITY PUBLISHING
1094 New DeHaven Street, Suite 100
West Conshohocken, PA 19428-2713
Toll-free (877) BUY BOOK
Local Phone (610) 941-9999
Fax (610) 941-9959
Info@buybooksontheweb.com
www.buybooksontheweb.com

58 Collected Poems of Richard W. Moyer

An Introduction *by Tree Riesener*	1
A Cat at the Battle of Waterloo	5
Straight Up	6
A Murad Cigarette	7
A Victim of Bernie Madoff Speaks	8
A Yacht	9
Absent-Minded	10
Airport	11
All That Money	12
An Advertising Executive Runs the Cross Country	13
Artillery Practice	14
At the End of the Garden	15
Aunt Alicia	16
Aunt Jane's Depression	17
Bernie Madoff	18
Can I Find a Red Woman?	19
Cynthia	20
Dancing With Grandfather	21
Deliverance	22
Depression	23
Regulator Johnson	24
February Spring	25
Feline Portrait	26
Gigolo	27
Gorgeous Blonde	28
Grim Ending	29
Hard Times	30
Where We Stand	31

March	32
Michael Vick	33
Chocolate Cake	34
Estate Planning	35
Fragments	36
In Memoriam—Dudley L. Thompson	37
Early Spring	38
The Score	39
The James Bond Syndrome	40
Palm Beach Dinner Party	41
One Quarter of a Gram	42
What Were They Thinking About?	43
Red Paint	44
Red	45
Movies, Youngstown, Ohio, 1940	46
My Days of Wine and Roses	47
Political Advice	48
My Psychiatrist	49
New Home	50
No Entrance	51
Remembering	52
Sir Allen Stanford	53
Scarsdale	54
Speculators at Lunch	55
Retail	56
What Was I Thinking About?	57
Welcome to Auschwitz*	58
Pastime	59
The Popcorn Stand	60
Small Talk	61
I Wonder?	62
Credits	63

58 Collected Poems by Richard W. Moyer

An Introduction by Tree Riesener

You have only to look at the titles of poems by Richard Moyer to know you are in a place as well defined as Faulkner's Yoknapatopha County, as Flannery O'Conner's doom-drenched south, as John Cheever's gin-drinking suburbs.

From the world of those who attend Harvard and sail yachts, wear Gisetta dresses and Gromondi boots, come such poems as "A Victim of Bernie Madoff Speaks," "An Advertising Executive Runs the Cross Country," "Grim Ending," "Hard Times," "My Days of Wine and Roses," and "My Psychiatrist."

However, far from being poems of cheerful consumption, these are grim poems by a man who has been in a lot of interesting places and observed with a keen eye. The poems derive their tone from the details he chooses to remember.

Therefore in "At the End of the Garden," behind ivy and roses on a white brick wall, waves swirl around jagged rocks. Suburbanites deal with groceries and medical appointments but also with tarantulas and typhoons. Delighting in the exhilaration of challenging downhill runs amidst mounds of snow and fogged-in mountains, his subjects dull their inner longings with pot and Jack Daniels. In "Hard Times," the wealthy guy next door, President of Turco Builders, puts a bullet in his brain. In "Artillery Practice," a bucolic green hill with warbling birds is "a perfect target for an artillery barrage."

This is a world where losing the nice tweed jacket you were arrested in is a greater tragedy than the arrest for drugs and rape, where even in an architect-renovated country house, "demons jump out of the woodwork."

Grim poems but always lilting, Richard Moyer's dance macabre is darkly jolly. In "A Yacht," the captain drinks a beer, a blonde sunbathes, two men play gin rummy and discuss the stock market while "about two miles away, a sloop with a black sail tacks toward the yacht." In "Aunt Alicia," a critical elderly woman cared for by six nurses complains endlessly about her dead husband, her unloving mother and daughter, until she dies of a stroke while eating a spoonful of oatmeal.

Yet the worth of these poems is not their blackly humorous portrayals of death and suffering visited on the unsuspecting but in their small touches of grace. As Moyer assesses cheating, illness, and murder, in "March," he prays that warm rain will fall. In "Welcome to Auschwitz," those waiting for death escape for a moment to contemplate pink and white blossoms, to sing a lullaby. In "Youngstown, Ohio," he remembers baseball scores and childhood's chocolate sundaes and whipped cream, the important things to a small boy living just after the Great Depression and just before America's entry into WWII.

This is sardonic work, even sarcastic, but underpinned by tenderness and grace. There are notes of hope—nothing grand or even redeeming, but the small hopes that get many of us through the day. There is fresh air at the end of the garden. You can return to an unfettered state by somersaulting in green valleys and painting pictures on rocks. A man paints himself red (with paint from Home Depot) and looks for an equally audacious woman. At 69, the narrator is in excellent shape. The diabetic happily goes into a coma to pay for his brief orgy with chocolate cake. "In Memoriam—Dudley L. Thompson" is a nod of acknowledgement to a business man who has worked honestly and unrecognized for his stockholders. Fleeting and small are these bits of hope. You have to search but in the midst of so many poems of stark, pain-filled reality, you're happy to find them.

Richard Moyer understands exactly what A.E. Houseman meant when he wrote about the soldier sliding off his opponent's sword, who "laughed and kissed his hand to me and died." If you're involved with life, living the common life of quiet desperation Thoreau wrote about, if you need a reminder that there can be grace in the grimmest of circumstances, read *58 Collected Poems* by Richard Moyer. You owe it to yourself!

Tree Riesener is a poet and fiction writer. Her published works include Liminalog, Angel Poison, *and* Inscapes. *A collection of ekphrastic poetry,* EK, *will be published by Cervena Barva Press in 2012.*

A Cat at the Battle of Waterloo

The roar of cannon,
smell of smoke,
moans and cries,
Napoleon's brigadier's hat droops on his head,
a look of desperation on his face,
he flourishes his sword in the air,
the silver steel flashes,
he curses Wellington;
a messenger gallops up with news of the battle
while you crouch behind a mound of earth,
your claws dig in,
your eyes shift from side to side,
your tail waves frantically,
you wail and wail
as if the end of the world has come.

Straight Up

the hill
on a sandy path
in Acadia National Park
overlooking the ocean,
the hamstrings of both my legs burn,
the corn on my right toe stiffens.
I continue to walk
slowly upward
as I see my rental car,
a silver Mercury Sable,
parked up the hill
100 yards away,
a place to sit down,
to remind myself that
at almost 69
I'm still
in excellent shape.

A Murad Cigarette

was misrepresented to me
by my roommate Peter Sperling in my
Freshman year at Harvard. There was
much discussion about opium, oriental
cigarettes, marijuana. I was approached
by Peter who said he had just gotten a
small shipment of opium cigarettes from
Istanbul. "Dick, I'll give you one but
they're very potent." That evening he
gave me a slender cigarette. Frightened,
I went outside the dormitory, stood against
a large tree, lit the cigarette and inhaled.
Peter leaned out the window and yelled
"Watch out Dick!" I inhaled deeply;
smoke came slowly out of my mouth.
I staggered forward. "Peter, Peter," I
screamed, "I'm drugged! I'm drugged!"
My whole body felt limp. From above,
laughter! Peter and my other two roommates
were hanging out of the window pointing
at me. Later I found out they had given me
a Murad cigarette, bought at a local tobacco shop.

A Victim of Bernie Madoff Speaks

I believed in Bernie.
He had been President of the Nasdaq and
owned a successful trading business.
He was angry if a dab of mustard fell
on the carpet in his office;
was insistent that his employees be
polite and soft-spoken;
dress in Armani suits and Laurent dresses.
He lunched with SEC regulators.
Bernie was an observant Jew,
a quality that appealed to me.
He contributed $20,000 every three months
to Temple Har Zion;
always prayed all day on Yom Kippur;
put a hand-carved mezuzah from Israel
on the door of his apartment;
sent cards to friends and neighbors on all the holidays;
made sure to kiss the Rabbi's wife on the cheek,
telling her she was what a Jewish wife should be.
The Rabbi was lucky to have her.

How could he be a crook?

A Yacht

In the Caribbean,
the captain at the wheel,
drinks a beer,
shouts at a sailor,
"hoist the mainsail!"
A blonde
with a blue sun visor,
body swathed in white lotion,
sunbathes on the foredeck.
Below,
two men with beards
discuss the stock market
as they play gin rummy.
In the galley the cook curses
as he drops an egg on the floor.
About two miles away
a sloop with black sail
tacks toward the yacht.

Absent-Minded

My watch often disappears and
I look in my cocker spaniel's mouth
I look in my clothes closet and examine
the pockets of a dozen suit coats
and a dozen sports jackets before
finding it in a formal black shoe where
I apparently placed it while taking off my tuxedo
after the annual Woodmen's Ball at The Forest Club.
I add up the cost of my absent-mindedness
not in dollars because most of the time
I find what I am looking for.
It's the trauma of having to
worry about where everything is.
I figure that someday I'll have a heart attack
while looking for the studs to my formal shirt.

Airport

Mothers push babies in strollers.
A boy in a yellow jacket with the motto
"Go Pink Panthers!" on it
gobbles a piece of pizza.
Two teenage girls,
out of their tank tops,
laugh as they pour cans of Diet Coke
down their throats.
Loudspeakers blare:
"American Flight 604 leaving from gate 29.
Continental Flight 201 delayed for one hour."
In the security zone a policeman
talks to a man
wearing a turban who fiddles
with a tiny metal object in his hand.
A white-haired man pulls a small bag
on rollers.
Men and women sit and read Time, The
Daily News, Ebony and Sports Illustrated.
In a secluded corner of the men's restroom
a flight attendant examines a silver bracelet
he picked up from the floor of an airplane.

All That Money

He was kind to his household help,
giving them gifts, seeing they were
housed in comfortable apartments.
Working for Bernie Madoff was
like working for Santa Claus.
Yeshiva University loved him;
all those scholarships paid for
by his brilliant investing.
Never mind that Yeshiva didn't know
what their money was invested in or
whether it was part of a Ponzi scheme,
the important thing was that money
rolled in month after month, year after year.
Rich folk in Palm Beach and Palm Springs
and a few on the French Riviera were happy.
Bernie financed their yachts, golf club memberships,
gambling losses at Monte Carlo and divorce settlements
until finally he had to admit he was a fraud and
he left them with nothing.

An Advertising Executive Runs the Cross Country

Miles of running
up and
down hills;
mud on my legs,
my arms pump,
my body
about to fall apart,
my eyes,
almost blinded
by sweat
my feet pounding
on macadam,
brick,
sand,
cement, grass;
the constant
pressure of
my competitors,
at my heels,
panting,
pushing,
grunting,
stumbling,
tearing sweat
off their faces;
so I
widen my stride,
run, run,
until I cross
the finish line,
ready to collapse,
the winner.

(Reminds me of competing for the
 Proctor and Gamble account.)

(Our Art Director is sleeping with a
 high-level Proctor and Gamble
 executive.)

(Our competitors are trying to hack
 into our computer system and find
 out what our plans are for Proctor
 and Gamble.)

(They're hiring private detectives to
 spy on us.)

(Just like our competitors for the
 Proctor and Gamble account.)

(The Proctor and Gamble account is
 worth $100,000,000.)

(I could be fired if we don't land the
 Proctor and Gamble account.)

(If I'm fired, could I become a cross
 country coach?)

(My twin sons are heavy pot users and
 flunking out of college.)
(My wife and I fight all the time. If I get
 a divorce I'll have to pay child support
 and 3 million dollars to my wife.)

Artillery Practice

A green hill
With warbling birds,
A perfect target
For an artillery barrage

At the End of the Garden

Roses,
ivy on a white brick wall
in front of
a 200 foot drop
to the ocean where
waves swirl
around jagged rocks
onto a sandy beach
with brown pebbles.
Seagulls cry and fly;
perch atop the wall.
The sun gleams on white brick.

The air is fresh.

Aunt Alicia

At seventy,
suspicious;
Her husband dead;
Her daughter moved away.
She hired an attorney
who hired a head nurse
who hired six nurses to
wait on her
seven days a week.
They fed her;
took her temperature;
bathed her;
listened to her complaints about
how life had deceived her;
how her husband was a lousy lover;
how she had an unloving mother
and daughter.

One day she had a massive stroke
while eating a spoonful of oatmeal.

Aunt Jane's Depression

Before I was married,
I thought depression was serious.
You went mad and tried to
jump out of a window.
Once I heard of a man
who pulled a gun from
a dusty closet shelf.
A friend of mine, a young scientist,
slashed his wrists in the bathtub.

Aunt Jane's symptoms are different.
She weeps and wails;
accuses her daughter of being unloving;
calls her sons' wives bitches;
commands her maid to
bring all her meals to her room;
then phones her psychiatrist,
orders him to ignore his other patients
and hurry to her.

When you are wealthy
depression counts.
It's easy to cheer up;
you add a new wing to your house;
change lawyers; go to the Riviera
or build a new swimming pool
with a marble lion that squirts water
from his mouth.

Bernie Madoff

knew-
if you promised clients
an average return of 1% a month
over a period of ten years
that rich people would invest with you.
Cause wealthy folks need lots of money.
It's expensive to own two homes, a
penthouse in Manhattan, a yacht and
a private jet.
7%to 10% return a year on
conservative investments might force you
to sell your yacht or penthouse.
So-you went to charming Bernie and
he took everything away.

Can I Find a Red Woman?

I think of red,
red socks,
red jackets,
red underwear;
I think of red till
I am giddy in
the head.
Red moves thru
my brain just as
red blood flows thru
my veins.
I am a totally red man
and wonder if
I can ever find
a totally red woman.

Cynthia

twists her hips,
swings her legs,
big breasts bob up and down.
Watching her excites me!
I shift from side to side,
my feet tap to the rhythm,
my eyes bulge,
my mind goes blank!
My God,
Cynthia really can dance.

Dancing With Grandfather

I'm invited to dance at a New Year's Eve party
by a 25 year-old brunette.
The band is playing the jungle bongo.
We throw our hands in the air!
We shout Happy New Year!
She is twisting her body with effortless ease;
her slim legs moving with grace
while I feel muscle pain
as I try to keep pace.
As we walk to our table
she says to me,
"My grandfather I never knew!
Now I've danced with a handsome granddad!
      Thank you!"

Deliverance

Oh for life on a remote tropical island!
No need to worry about
    Terrorists
    The IRS
    Your mother-in-law
    Your children's education
    The grocery store
    Computer failure
    Personal liability insurance
    Incessant calls from your lawyer
    doctor, dentist and accountant
    Traffic jams
    Expensive prescription drugs
    Extensive wardrobe
    Big veterinary bills
    Country club dues
    but you, your family and pets
    will need to know
    how to deal with tarantulas, typhoons
    and head hunters.

Depression

You sit in a chair
and stare.
You cry
when your favorite team
scores a touchdown on TV.
You can't move your legs
or respond to
your wife's kiss which
ordinarily makes you feel
wonderful, but now burns
like dry ice
on your cheek.

Regulator Johnson

A cloudy day,
A mountain fogged in;
big mounds of snow beckoned him.
Shunning an easy slope,
he strapped his long skis on;
chose Regulator Johnson,
icy, steep
with moguls six feet deep.
He pushed off on his skis;
his body started to sweat.
He rose and fell;
he skied on.
This was an exhausting way.
Was he playing tennis
with Bjorn Borg
on clay?
He came to the bottom;
his soul on fire;
he'd brag about this feat for years
and not be a liar.

February Spring

What's this!
Tulips in February!
I could sunbathe,
play tennis,
put the top down!
Are the seasons reversing?
Will I ski in July?
Go to Florida
to escape
the summer cold!

Feline Portrait

My black and white cat
stands beside a brown pond,
his tail, a thin sword.

My cat is still.
The pond is still.
The summer air is heavy.

Gigolo

All you know is your trade
of wine, touch, flattery,
 ultimate pleasure.
Your client is excited,
may even truly like you
while you mouth trite words
of passion.
You're sure you don't need
real intimacy.
Alone,
you dull inner longings
with pot and Jack Daniels,
turn on the TV to
a Celtics game..

Gorgeous Blonde

walking down Fifth Avenue
with glittering gold earrings,
Gisetta dress,
Gromondi boots,
Gromoto leather hand bag-
 I wonder-
Are you married to a wealthy lawyer?
How often do you and your husband have sex?
Have you ever had an affair?
Was it with another lawyer in your husband's office?
Did you consider marrying him?
Did you ever snort cocaine or smoke pot?
Did you invest with Bernie Madoff?

Grim Ending

What if they
open me up and find
the tumor is inoperable
or the condition
of my blood vessels
so bad that
no surgeon can operate or
they can take out the tumor but
the cancer has spread and
I've only got six months
and chemotherapy
is a real long shot and
I feel like a sailor
trapped below deck
on a sinking ship.

Hard Times

My sixty-year old aunt survives
by selling her antique jewelry.
My cousin, once an accountant at AIG,
has been drawing unemployment benefits
for a year.
I owe $50,000 on credit cards;
my wife wants a divorce;
my business almost bankrupt.
Last night, the guy next door,
President of Turco Builders,
put a bullet through his brain.

Where We Stand

There is no light
at the end of childhood,
only years of work.
What will we become?
We have high hopes
for our lives but
grapple with daily routine
that has no dramatic vision.
There are moments when
we want to climb,
breathe fresh air,
stand naked on
a rocky peak,
somersault in
the green valleys below,
paint pictures on rocks.

March

Barren hills merge
into cloudy skies;
the land is frozen.
Atop a fallen oak
I stand
and hear
a robin chirping.
I pray that
warm rain
falls
soon.

Michael Vick

Why the Eagles for Michael Vick?
Eagles: birds of majesty and freedom;
Michael Vick: dogs in the pit
trying to tear each other apart.

Chocolate Cake

Sneak into kitchen,
wolf double chocolate cake,
tastes fantastic;
makes sugar-starved
diabetic me-
happy!

Go into a coma;
ambulance comes;
off to the hospital;
big shot of insulin;
from now on-
asparagus and artichoke diet!

Estate Planning

Death is certain.
How you leave
your money
is not.
Think about it now.
When you're in the grave,
it's over and under.

Fragments

From my window
completely brown
rocks stand silent
one bullet
a dead wife
a blue jay
soft April grass
the sun flames
a car radio
the Star Spangled Banner
the green leaves of May
in your sweet little Alice blue gown.

In Memoriam — Dudley L. Thompson

How often you sat
at your old wooden desk
using a 1945 calculator.
Years later,
when you sold the business
for a sum 243 times greater than
what you paid for it,
did your stockholders realize
what you did for them or
were they too busy
sailing, golfing, skiing,
traveling abroad or
building new homes.

Early Spring

My new furnace and
air purifier kept me
from catching colds,
or getting the flu
while proper use
of rock salt stopped me
from slipping on ice and
breaking my neck.
I forgot about Iraq,
my stocks,
the housing market,
the price of oil,
a possible depression.

Now it's spring;
flowers bloom, birds sing;
my economic self stirs;
a sense of disaster grips me.
What will happen to the housing market?
Can Iraq become a viable nation?
Where will my stocks go?
Will the country go into a deep recession?
What price for a gallon of gas?
Then there's the arthritis in my spine
which prevents me from walking two blocks
without terrible pain in my hips!

The Score

A gray-haired man wearing a red cap
slops up beer from a giant red cup.
It dribbles down a red vest
that says "Go Red Bears!"

A young woman, blonde hair in a bob,
sits next to her husband who curses when
the Red Bear quarterback gets sacked
or throws an incomplete pass..
She glances at the field,
then goes back to reading "Scarlet, Sequel
to Gone With the Wind".

.The Red Bears score on a long pass.
The Red Bear quarterback jumps on the end
who caught the pass.
They dance about in joyous embrace.

Everyone with a red vest, red banner, red-painted chest
screams and stomps,
throws their arms in the air,
kisses their date.

The blonde reads a sexy passage and chuckles.
Near an exit a youth in blue jeans snatches the wallet
of a six foot five man.

The James Bond Syndrome

How many times have you seen a James Bond movie
and asked yourself why you went in the first place?
Why are you fascinated with the athletic James who
outruns the bad guys, makes love to the heroine
on a majestic yacht on a king-size bed
with a gold headboard, a dark green emerald in it?
Is your own life so dull? Maybe it's your wife always
cooking turkey with dressing, hamburgers,
brussel sprouts, carrots and peas?
Maybe you don't have enough money or skill
to ski down mountains in pursuit of a bad guy
who has the combination to a Swiss bank account
in his backpack that he intends to use to buy
an atomic bomb that will destroy Chicago.

You're probably tired of sex on Monday,
paying the bills on Tuesday, dining out with
your wife's parents on Thursday.
Hey, just think, James gets tired too, running
from one bed to another with a blonde, brunette
or redhead.
Look at all those weights he must lift to stay in shape,
all the B-12 shots to give him extra energy.
Then he gets shot at, hit over the head
with baseball bats, beaten with rubber truncheons,
stabbed by the blonde villainess he slept with,
not to speak of having to deal with M who
sends him on one deadly mission after another and
doesn't put any money into his 401K.

.

Palm Beach Dinner Party

    The flash of
        diamonds
Drum rhythm
Givenchy gowns
Conversation:
"Christina's fried apple tarts
        cause horrible
        indigestion.
Earl Smythe-Jones
        is
the finest divorce lawyer
        in
South Florida and only
        charges
$5,000 an hour.
The Episcopal minister
Joel Van Rittingham is
        gay.
Lillian Braithwaite does
social work in
the slums of
        Miami
twice a week."

One Quarter of a Gram

of Marijuana
found in the bottom of the
side pocket in your tweed
sports jacket can really get you
in big trouble. The sixty-year-old
judge in criminal court who
goes to church every Sunday
will throw the book at you.
In his mind he is doing God's will.
You'll get on a criminal list that
will make you an unwanted neighbor;
put you in league with
Mexican drug lords, Bernie Madoff,
men who have raped five women,
two of them underage.
You may even have to report to
a parole officer and have
mandatory counseling.
People will shun you!
You won't be employed by
many businesses. law firms, schools.
What's worse, the law will seize
your jacket as evidence. You will
never see it again.

What Were They Thinking About?

The president of a firm waits four months
to fire a dishonest subordinate.
A cancer patient, needing chemotherapy to live
delays treatment for half a year.
A housewife refuses to
open her credit card bills
for five months.
A firm facing bankruptcy
goes on paying big salaries
to top executives.
A Prime Minister decides to negotiate
with a tyrant rather than being tough with him
and stop the second world war!

Red Paint

Red jackets
Red socks
Red underwear
I think of red till I am giddy in the head.
Red moves thru my brain
just as red blood flows thru my veins.
Tomorrow I'm going down to Home Depot,
buy the most outrageous shade of red
and paint myself red from head to toe.

Red

I think of red,
red socks,
red jackets,
red underwear;
I think of red till
I am giddy in
the head.
Red moves thru
my brain just as
red blood flows thru
my veins.
I am
a totally
red man and
wonder if
I can ever find
a totally
red woman
to love.

Movies, Youngstown, Ohio, 1940

We took seats in the balcony, first row,
talked about the Rayen Tigers,
Slingin Sammy Baugh.
Just the week before, his 50 yard touchdown strike
beat Cleveland 21 to 20 in the last 30 seconds of play.
Wasn't he the best quarterback in the NFL?.
Abbot and Costello on the screen,
discussing baseball;
"Who's on first?" Abbott would ask Costello
and fat Lou would answer, "Smith and Jones are on
second and third." "Yes, yes", Abbott would reply,
"But who's on first?"
Tarzan saved Jane from alligators.
His "OOOOh" cry almost shattered our eardrums.
After the movies we walked next door to Smith's Ice Cream
parlor;
30˘ for a chocolate sundae
with whipped cream., nuts and cherry.
Mrs. Smith served us,
a round badge on her lapel read
"Re-elect Roosevelt in 1940!"

My Days of Wine and Roses

were all of two consecutive Saturdays
in my freshman year at Harvard.
Energized by the thought
of wine, women and song
I decided to
experiment with Dutch Genever Bols,
one of the hottest gins
ever invented.
On two consecutive Saturdays
I got tanked up,
my roommates encouraging me
to take one glass more;
after half a bottle,
I was fired up,
ran out to the Harvard Yard
singing Harvard fight songs,
staggering along the brick sidewalks,
admonishing other students
to weep no more,
get laid.
I returned to my room
where I fell into the shower
with my clothes on
and spent the next hour
singing Frankie Lane's "Mule Train"
as loud as possible.
I would yell "Mule Train, Yah"
and from above
a pounding on the ceiling,
a voice yelled,
"Shut up! Shut up!"

Political Advice

You can't get elected
selling peace
unless there's prosperity too.
So--go to war
against a tyrant
you can beat.
Order lots of military hardware;
employ lots of people.
Have the central bank
keep interest rates low.

People will buy condominiums
with no down payment.
Max out their credit cards
on Mazdas, Maytags and
diamonds on the internet.

Forget that millions
of citizens have
no health insurance
or retirement funds.

For God's sake
keep the economy moving.

My Psychiatrist

sits in a large armchair
a pipe in his mouth,
smoke slowly rising from it.
He listens,
looks at me,
as if he was watching a boring movie.

I recount my early years,
my failure--
to run an ice cream stand!
My F in Calculus!

He just sits,
face blank.
Smoke floats upward.
He shrugs his shoulders,
says, "Hmm, same time next week?"

New Home

My wife and I feel cramped
in our small home in the country.
A prominent architect
presents a plan,
recommends a builder
and a New York decorator
who tell us they will create
a Town and Country estate.

Two years later;
the windows stick,
the furnace whines,
water seeps onto our pantry floor.
The purple paint in our new dining room
glares so we wear sunglasses
to the dinner table.

My wife goes to a psychiatrist.
Nothing halts my ulcer.
Our dog Winnie used to walk erect.
Now she slouches, glances warily,
looks for demons to jump out of the woodwork.

No Entrance

Frightened by thunder,
lightning and sheets of rain
the black cat dashes
for the locked front door
of the house.
Inside-
a redhead,
stripped to her underwear,
drinks martinis,
dances to bongo music,
leans on the chest of
a six-foot-three man,
a joint
in the side
of his mouth.
The cat wails
and scratches the door!

Remembering

the year I went Scuba diving
at St. Maartens
and couldn't see anything;
the sea surged;
all the fish disappeared;
all the bright tropicals
replaced by specks of white sand
and great disappointment
because I'd read about exotic reefs;
angelfish, guppies, silverfish,
gills opening and closing,
darting in and out of caves
in a mountainous tropical reef.

Sir Allen Stanford

Oh, he is a worthy man,
knighted by the crown;
a man of great civic pride,
he sponsored a local soccer team,
won tournaments.
Oh, he is a good citizen of Antigua,
raised the average income from
from $7,000 to $11,000 a year
with his bank and investment business
that brought in over a billion dollars
in deposits;

Oh, he is a crook who
stole over 2 billion dollars
selling investors phony CD'S and
other bogus investment packages.
Then he disappeared.
Where did the money go?
Where is Allen Stanford, a knight without honor?

Scarsdale

In a tearoom I met a friend;

    he told me of a paradise

where massive houses with room-length couches

    stand

in a world of green manicured lawns.

    I sat for a moment,

        then,

    impelled to speak,

        I stopped

and ordered a cup of tea.

Speculators at Lunch

Well aren't you a bunch of mean-assed
honchos, all dressed up in St. Vincent suits and
Saragand ties, looking to make millions on bank
failures and oil futures. You sit around drinking
Old Fashioneds, figuring out how to short stocks
you don't own, what hedge fund to own, when to
buy platinum on the margin and make a ton of
dough, even if you help disrupt the entire US
financial system. You claim you're keeping the
markets honest. Instead you're looking for
a lot of extra bucks to purchase a yacht, buy a
grandmaster painting at Sotheby's and
give your wife a crummy divorce settlement
so you can marry your twenty-five year old mistress.

Retail

Starting at nine a.m.
going on to seven , eight
or even nine p.m.,
I wait on customers,
check on inventory,
make computer entries as to what
is selling and what is not
until sometimes I can't tell
the difference between a
pink brassiere and a pair
of high-heeled shoes and
I have to note if the fashion
is changing because it could
be economic disaster if I
am heavy on white tights,
and short orange skirts become the rage
or the formal look returns
and it's out the window with short dresses
and slender silver bracelets which cost
me $200 each.
I am left with thousands of dollars of inventory
and no buyers.

What Was I Thinking About?

At sixty
misread the invitation;
went to a formal wedding
in blue suit, shirt and a tie
with a picture of a hound dog
on it; all the other men in
black tuxedos and white bow ties.
I sat in the back row.

At seventy-one
how could I not realize
that the lift stopped
at two levels?
I sat in the chair--
too long; got off
too late.
The chair swerved
to the next level;
threw me down;
smashed my left hand
on a steel pole;
broke my back;
ending my skiing career.

Welcome to Auschwitz*

The sun shines.
A band plays a Strauss waltz
for the arriving prisoners.
Children are given chocolates.
A mother sings a lullaby
to a baby in her arms.
Pink and white blossoms
fall from the trees.
Relieved, for a moment-
men, women and children
forget being pushed into line
by Nazi bayonets;
forget the hundreds that starved
to death in the cattle cars that
carried them here;
ignore the warning from the column
of white smoke in the distance!

*Auschwitz was the concentration camp in which millions of Jews were gassed and then cremated; their ashes rising, white in the sky.

Pastime

To stand
at
my window
watching geese
eating grass
honking.

The Popcorn Stand

At the Cineplex
watch the popcorn man
at the popcorn stand.
In one corner of the lobby
four girls
clap their hands
and giggle.
Near the stand,
two young men,
arms waving,
argue about the
Temple basketball team;
people shuffle in a long line,
push each other
to see a popular film.
The popcorn man
moves just enough
to sell
a bag of popcorn.

Small Talk

"Nassau was so nice!" she said,
calmly pushing her skirt below her knees
and smiling slyly at the gentleman
next to her,
"but we were thrilled with Montego Bay,
such a dazzling place, so gay,
so charming with its deluxe hotels
and exquisite service."
The room buzzed
and so did its people,
talking of Montego Bay
and Nassau and Bermuda
and Palm Beach and what
jewelry and dresses
they had bought and
all the splendid greens
and tennis courts and
the people worth knowing
they had met
and the exquisite service
at the Hotel
dela Coba Caravanserai.

I Wonder?

Do I waddle through life?
Do I honk at strangers
and friends?
When at night
I dream of
a graceful swan
gliding on a pond,
in harmony
with nature.
I wonder,
am I a goose or
a swan?

Credits

A Cat at the Battle of Waterloo reprinted courtesy of Free Verse magazine

Straight Up reprinted courtesy of Ibbetson Street Press

An Advertising Executive Runs the Cross Country reprinted courtesy of the Endicott Review

Artillery Practice reprinted courtesy of the Endicott Review

Feline Portrait reprinted courtesy of Free Verse

Grim Ending reprinted courtesy of Nerve Cowboy

Movies, Youngstown, Ohio, 1940 reprinted courtesy of the Endicott Review

A Murad Cigarette reprinted courtesy of the Endicott Review

My Psychiatrist reprinted courtesy of the Mad Poets Review

No Entrance reprinted courtesy of Nerve Cowboy

What Was I Thinking About reprinted courtesy of Free Verse

Absent-Minded reprinted courtesy of Verse Wisconsin

Aunt Jane's Depression reprinted courtesy of Fight These Bastards

Cynthia reprinted courtesy of The Poet

Deliverance reprinted courtesy of Verse Wisconsin

Depression reprinted courtesy of Mad Poets Review

Fragments reprinted courtesy of The Cancer Center - A Chapbook

Early Spring reprinted courtesy of Free Verse

Red Paint reprinted courtesy of the Pink Cadillac

Pastime reprinted courtesy of the Pink Cadillac